DUNDEE

... the way it was

DUNDEE

... the way it was

Douglas Phillips and Ron Thompson

Illustrations © Douglas Phillips
Text   © Ron Thompson
Printed and published by David Winter & Son Ltd
Unit 16, Dunsinane Avenue, Dunsinane Industrial Estate, Dundee
First printed August 1991
This edition re-printed September 1993

ISBN 0 902804 21 9

DOUG PHILLIPS

Doug Phillips' work as an artist has been recognised world-wide. His paintings have been reproduced on the front cover of Readers Digest and his drawings have illustrated over a hundred children's books in Britain and the U.S.A. His oils and watercolours are regularly hung at the exhibitions of the Royal Scottish Academy, the Glasgow Institute of Fine Art, and the Royal Scottish Society of Painters in Watercolour. Several of his paintings have become limited edition prints. He started work as an office boy in a Dundee jute factory.

RON THOMPSON

Ron Thompson has been a journalist for over forty years. He began with D.C. Thomson and later worked on various national newspapers, including the "Daily Herald" and the "Sunday Express," before joining Grampian Television as their Dundee-based reporter in 1965. After 26 years in front of the camera he is now a freelance writer and broadcaster. He is author of "Never A Dull Moment," an account of his early adventures in television, and of "Beyond 2001," the story of an engineer who invented a space machine in his garden shed. He, too, began his working life as an office boy in a local jute firm.

Phillips.

The High Street and Nethergate Dundee.
1950's

INTRODUCTION

During the past thirty years Dundee has possibly undergone greater physical change than any other city in Scotland. Entire precincts have been bulldozed into oblivion . . . landmarks have disappeared . . . the character of the old town has been altered beyond recognition. Much of the swagger has deserted the step of what was once the jute capital of the world. Since 1962 the old Overgate, the Wellgate, most of Hawkhill, parts of Blackness Road and Victoria Road, and sections of the High Street and Nethergate, have gone for ever. The West Station, the Royal Arch, and the patchwork of docks which brought the harbour lapping into the very heart of the city, have been obliterated. So, too, have over 30 cinemas. Even as I write a squadron of mechanical diggers is blazing a trail across the foot of the Hilltown, carving out a concrete canyon for the final section of the inner ring road. The city has been revamped on a grand scale. But if such sweeping redevelopment has been inevitable so, also, is the overwhelming sense of nostalgia created in its wake for all the cherished places which have been taken from us. In this richly illustrated book, commemorating Dundee's 800th anniversary as a burgh, the popular artist, Douglas Phillips, a native Dundonian like myself, has lovingly recreated on his drawing board the city as it once was, providing an evocative journey into the past for those who can remember for themselves and, for those who can't, a delightful impression of the place we were in the first half of this century.

Ron Thompson,
August 1991

WHERE better to start our journey back through time than from the very heart of the city itself where the High Street broadens out, almost into a piazza, at the foot of Reform Street. Our lofted view to the west shows the High Street running into the Nethergate which then reaches out to the Perth Road while, on the right, the Overgate meanders up to meet the West Port. The skyline is dominated by the Old Steeple which, apart from the basic street pattern, is possibly Dundee's last surviving relic of the Middle Ages. This great tower gave final sanctuary to the town's governor, Robert Lumsden, who fled there on September 1, 1651, with a handful of supporters to provide a last pocket of resistance to the invading English army of General Monk. When the six-week battle finally ended several days later Lumsden was beheaded and Cromwell's men, rampaging through the streets, massacred 1200 civilians and stripped the town of all its assets. Following the orgy Monk billetted himself in the corner house with the round tower at the bottom of the Overgate. Latterly, and somewhat incongruously, the English general's former headquarters sat above the Sixty Minute Cleaners, overlooking a coffee stall towed into position each evening to refresh the city's revellers, loungers, and nightshift workers. The stall was kept supplied by local baker J. Murdoch Wallace, a kenspeckle figure of his time, who also opened the J.M. Ballroom in North Tay Street in 1954. His great ambition, however, was to gain a seat on Dundee Town Council and while Monk had secured power in the city in a matter of weeks, "Murdie" tried and failed for over 30 years, contesting more elections than possibly any other person in local municipal history. He even exploited a loophole in the law by once standing as a candidate in two wards at the same time and failing to win either. One of his distinguishing features was a Rolls Royce which could often be seen cruising along the High Street – although it was the tramcar that once dominated Dundee's main thoroughfare.

It was from here that the electric cars rocked and hummed their way towards suburbia, their destination boards bearing such proud names as Maryfield, West Park Road, Lochee, Blackness, Downfield, and Ninewells. Except for the wider Lochee trams which had normal seating, passengers sat facing each other on long, polished leather benches running the entire length of the car. The first tram route, using horse traction, was opened in August, 1877, between the Post Office and Dalhousie Terrace.

Steam trams were introduced in 1885, pulled by a power unit complete with chimney. The billowing smoke, and possibly burning cinders, made it necessary to roof over the top decks. But when electric cars first appeared on the scene in 1900 effluent was no longer a hazard and so they had a sporty look with open tops. But soon the roofs were back, this time due to the rigours of the climate, although small open verandas were often left at either end of the upper deck. In 1905 there was great controversy over whether the trams should run on a Sunday. Many people said they required such a service to attend church and following a plebescite, which voted in favour of Sabbath running, a seven-day timetable was brought into operation. After the Second World War, however, the vast new housing estates built across the northern perimeter of the city were far beyond the reach of the existing tracks. Finally, on a tear-filled night in October, 1956, the last tram ran from Maryfield to Lochee. Six years later the curtain also began to fall on much of central Dundee.

The High Street

Douglas Phillips.

IN the middle of the 18th century Dundee, now with a prosperous shipping trade, decided to push the boat out in a different sense. The council commissioned the famous Scottish Architect William Adam to design one of the finest civic buildings in the land, a town house that would reflect the city's growing importance as a manufacturing centre. The Pillars, as it became known because of the arched frontage, was built on the south side of the High Street in 1732, its spire rising to a hundred and forty feet. The opulent interior had a fine oval staircase and contained a council chamber, a guild hall, and numerous other apartments, several of which were allocated to the town clerk. Accommodation on the upper floor was at one time used as a jail. For two hundred years The Pillars was held in great affection, becoming the favourite rendezvous for people wishing to meet up in the centre of the town. It was ideal for this purpose because of the sheltered shopping arcade it provided at street level. But the building had been made from inferior stone and through time began to crumble, causing the fine, exterior ornamental work to disintegrate.

The Pillars and Old Town House. Dundee

Despite pleas from a strong sentimental lobby the old town house was pulled down in 1931, giving much-needed work to the unemployed and creating the generous space required for the City Square with its crowning glory of the Caird Hall. The present town house, or city chambers, was later built on the west side of the square facing over to the Cafe Val D'or. But in 1898 another historic building had appeared in the High Street, just across the road from The Pillars. Called, The Hub, it was reputed to be the smallest newsagent's shop in Britain, consisting simply of a counter placed across the foot of an old flight of stairs between Samuel's the jewellers and Young the tobacconist. The premises were not much bigger than a telephone kiosk and customers were forced to transact their business from the pavement. The owner gained entry by almost crawling through a small hatch in the counter. Like its more distinguished neighbour on the other side of the street, The Hub was sadly missed when it closed in 1960.

Just along the High Street, in stark contrast, was one of the city's biggest and grandest retail establishments, D.M. Brown's. This family department store, with old-fashioned elevators and genteel restaurant, possessed an air of grandness which was one of the hallmarks of up-market shopping before the advent of chain stores and supermarkets. In these days the assistant would very often put the bill with the money into a metal capsule which was then propelled by compressed air through a tube leading to a central cash desk on another floor, and from there your change would be sent back to the counter. A few doors away at William Millar, the grocer, there was a similar system of transacting business, except here they had a maze of wires instead of tubes criss-crossing their way up to the office in a gallery overlooking the main floor. The assistant simply pulled a lever and the steel container zoomed off into space like a cable car. G.L. Wilson's, Smith Brothers, Draffens, Caird's, Justice . . . like "D.M's", they all had a touch of class and personal service which no longer has the same priority in the new order of High Street trading.

Overgate Dundee.

O F all the old haunts which Dundonians pine for it is the Overgate that dominates their sense of nostalgia. Here, in the very heart of the city, was a world of infinite variety, a congestion of tumbledown tenements providing shops, houses, pubs, restaurants, colourful characters, quaint landmarks, and strange customs. The Overgate, more than any other place, exuded a jolly, bustling, almost carnival atmosphere. Even those who didn't live there felt at home in its presence. But it wasn't always like this. In much earlier times the Overgate accommodated the aristocracy; the Marquis of Argyll, the Viscount of Dundee, the Earls of Angus, the Duke and Duchess of Buccleugh and Monmouth. Later the mansions were occupied by the merchant princes and captains of industry. But during the 1800's, when Dundee's population multiplied almost six-fold from 30,000 to 170,000 with the city's burgeoning textile industry, the rich built their swagger houses on the outskirts and the increasing numbers of poor gradually took over the inner city. During the first half of this century the Overgate also became one of Dundee's busiest and most popular shopping areas. Here you could buy anything from fashionable footwear to a ha'penny-worth of milk in a special poke. There was the Tom Thumb fruit bazaar, Franchi's restaurant, Wallace's tea room, the Beef Can Close, pawn shops galore, and Greenhills, the chemist, where they concocted a cure-all drink called Sarsparilla. The strong stuff was served up in a host of convivial taverns beloved by their patrons; the Mercat Cross, the Variety Bar, The Pump, the Harp and Thistle, the Star, Parliamentary Bar, Steeple Bar . . . The Overgate, the pub capital of Dundee, had this characteristic, and many others too, immortalised in verse and song:

"Oh, as Eh went doon the Overgate,
Eh met wee Johnny Scobie,
He says tae me 'Dae ye tak a half'?,
Says Eh 'Man, that's meh hoabby'"!

On a Saturday night the gaslit Overgate became a clamorous, garish fairground with sideshows promising such exotic delights as "The World's Greatest Flea Circus", "The Dancing Cannibals from Borneo", "The Tallest Woman in the World", and "Captain Wallace, Fire Eater". There was a Mexican knife thrower, predictably called Pedro Gonzales, whose target was a female assistant dressed as an Indian squaw. Captain Texas was a cowboy who lay on his back and with a .22 rifle would shatter a sugar cube on top of a cork sitting on the head of his daughter, little Dodo Texas. It was here, too, that you found most of the city's model lodging houses with "clean comfortable beds at 4d a night" being offered at Paddy Rock's, Machir's, and Turley's. At the flea circus in a shop at the corner of Long Wynd the insects, attached by fine silken threads to miniature coaches, were prodded into action by a ring master using a long, steel rod. What is more, the circus management claimed its performers were all Dundee fleas – bred and caught in Paddy Rock's lodging house! Then there was "The Poet's Box", run latterly by Lowden Macartney, where they offered "a million" songs, recitations, parodies and ballads in printed form at a penny a time. This was a favourite hunting ground for farm workers, wearing their caps or "doolichters" and looking for bothy ballads. When Dundee's Howff of Song put up the shutters in 1945 yet another facet of the city's character had been chipped away. Yes, there was no place quite like the Overgate. But long before the end it had degenerated into a scandalous slum, equalled only by the squalor of Glasgow's Gorbals. Those who lived there, or who had sampled its conditions, were glad to see it go.

> "Jist a wee bit but and half a ben,
> When I look back I aye wonder
> Hoo we a' lived I dinna ken,
> Wi' nine o' us crammed in yonder."

Top of The Overgate

THE Overgate was really a maze of closes, lanes, streets and wynds; a network of walkways which contributed much to the overall character of the area. Thorter Row, connecting to the High Street, was one of these thoroughfares. Within its short span you would find a grocer, fruiterer, barber, tobacconist, and the celebrated Cafe Royal bar whose eclectic clientele included artistes from the Palace Theatre, journalists, sporting figures and bookies' runners. But Thorter Row had a restricted outlook until the Whitehall area was developed towards the end of the 19th century. It was then that Whitehall Street was laid out directly opposite, on the other side of the High Street, running down to Whitehall Crescent where it centred on Gilfillan Memorial Church. So now when you stood in Thorter Row the vista had been dramatically extended to take in the fine architecture of the new street with the impressive frontage of the church rearing up at the bottom end.

The church was completed in 1888 and named after the Rev. George Gilfillan, who had died ten years earlier after a long and memorable ministry at the city's School Wynd Church. Gilfillan was an intellectual giant and powerful preacher with a natural, common touch, a man who fought bigotry with the same tenacity as he tended to the needs of his people. He was also a gifted writer with a prodiguous ouput of poetry and prose, as well as editing forty volumes of the work of other British poets. Gilfillan Church was later to prosper under the ministry of Harry Andrew throughout the Depression and the war that followed. His oratory, like Gilfillan's, had such spell-binding qualities that tickets had sometimes to be issued for his services. The building itself has lost its fine wooden cupola, the domed structure which rotted and had to be removed for safety reasons in 1958.

Rev. George Gilfillan

Rev. Harry Andrew

Thorter Row. Dundee.

Douglas Phillips.

Mid Kirk Style. Dundee

MID Kirk Style was a pleasant little backwater running between the main spine of the Overgate and the rear of the City Churches. On a Saturday it was transformed into an open-air market, packed with people browsing through a clutter of stalls in search of bargains. In a sense it was like a great big jumble sale. Here you could pick up almost anything from carpets, books, and odd rolls of wallpaper, to crockery, bicycles and bits of furniture. Even the odd key was available – with your ha'penny back if it didn't fit the lock when you reached home. And if your purchases were too bulky to carry you simply borrowed, or hired, a wheelbarrow to take them away. But what really gave Mid Kirk Style a touch of class on market days were the "busters". They were the great crowd pullers. Busters were simply a brimming plateful of peas and chips dished up with a savoury bree. The French no doubt would have dignified such an offering with a garnishing of fancy phrases. But to Dundonians a buster was a buster, a real tightener, a few coppersworth of simple fare that put you at peace with the world. The eating arrangements were also without frills.

The buster stall was nothing more than a big wooden shed with long forms round the walls. There was no door, simply an open entrance, and the roof was made from canvas which flapped about in the wind. The cooking was done in black pots on a big, fiercely-hot coke brazier in the middle of the stall in full view of the diners. In fact the preparation of certain dishes at the table in some fashionable restaurants may well owe its origin to the Dundee buster stalls! It is undoubtedly true, however, that in a city famous for its pies and bridies and slabs of cake, the buster held its own. On the last day of 1990, when the city centre was turned into a carnival for the official launch of Dundee's Octocentenary Year, the buster stalls were brought back for an encore and did a roaring trade. Mid Kirk Style ran off Tally Street where the fireplace specialists, Kirk and Coutts, had their premises right below the New Imperial Hotel. Other city centre hotels included the Royal in Union Street, the Royal British at the top of Castle Street, and Mather's, a temperance establishment, right across from the West Station.

The Royal and Mather's still operate, the latter under a different name, while the Royal British is now a university residence for students. The Imperial bit the dust with the rest of the Overgate precinct. But others have since appeared to take their place. The Angus Hotel has been a feature of the new Overgate since 1963 and more recently, in 1988, the Earl Grey rose from the site of the old dock of that name in the landfall area of the road bridge. These hotels are part of the new Dundee, helping to cope with the huge volume of visitors to the city each year.

South Lindsay St.
Dundee

Douglas Phillips.

THROUGHOUT its long and turbulent history Dundee has possibly been sacked, pillaged and destroyed more often than any other town in Scotland. But the one building which has defied all the forces of destruction is, appropriately, the most commanding edifice in the city – St. Mary's Tower, better known as the Old Steeple, rising to 156 feet and now the oldest surviving tower in Scotland. This square, massive Gothic building, with walls eight feet thick, stands at the western extremity of the city churches which were grouped together to form a cathedral-looking structure, the nave, transept, and chancel forming separate places of worship. Viewed here on the left from the foot of South Lindsay street and on the right from the top of the Overgate, the Old Steeple clearly presides over the centre of the city like an ancient guardian, the last remnant of 14th century Dundee. Built on the site of the original Church of St. Mary, which was destroyed in 1303 by Edward I of England, the tower withstood the onslaught of the Duke of Somerset's forces in 1547, followed by that of the Marquis of Montrose in 1645. Six years later it was spared in the scorched earth policy of General Monk, before finally surviving a devastating fire which gutted the churches in 1841 but left the Steeple standing, phoenix-like, as it is today. The churches were rebuilt immediately but the fire had disastrous consequences for the town's finances. During the previous thirteen years so much had been spent on repairing the building that little had been left to fully insure the churches.

The tower, which has two fine, lace-work galleries, was originally intended to have a crown. Instead, however, it was topped off with a small slated structure called a cape house, at one time used as a prison. Across the road from the Old Steeple, in South Lindsay Street, was another holy building, School Wynd Church of George Gilfillan fame, which latterly became Kidd's function rooms. Every Saturday evening Kidd's was the most popular place in town for young ballroom dancers. Quick-stepping round the crowded floor was the highlight of the week for hundreds of teenagers who later graduated to the more mature ballrooms of the Palais, Locarno, and Empress.

Phillips.
Overgate 1950s

Morgan Tower. Dundee.

ONE of the outstanding features of the Nethergate is Morgan Tower, an imposing circular building wedged into a row of tenements lining the street across from the Queen's Hotel. The tower may have been adapted from part of Dundee's old defensive wall, taking its present unique form in 1794 when it was owned by a local sea captain, Daniel Morgan, who ran the tower as a block of mansion flats, the role it still fulfils today under the ownership of a housing association. The bow-fronted Gothic structure has Venetian windows and an oriental-style roof, rather like a Saracen's helmet, reputed to have been features admired by Morgan on buildings he had studied during time spent in foreign parts. It is known, however, that these were also the design trademarks of Samuel Bell who had handled the Morgan Tower brief. Bell, formerly a craftsman, had become Dundee's first, and distinguished, town architect in 1772.

His other projects were to include the outstanding St. Andrew's Church in the Cowgate, the Trades Hall and the Union Hall in the High Street, and the Theatre Royal in Castle Street. Morgan's Buildings, as the tower was originally called, offered flats at an annual rental of £18.17.6d which included full use of cellars, attics, and courtyard well. In modern times the well and the cellars have never been located, although the latter could have occupied the ground-floor premises prior to them becoming a pharmacy in 1874, which they have remained ever since under five different owners. The chemist's shop was originally opened at the foot of the tower to serve the considerable number of doctors who at one time practised in this part of the town. Legend has it that Captain Morgan returns to his beloved tower every Christmas Eve for a quick look round, his arrival always signalled by the rustle of his haversack as he climbs the winding stairway at the rear of the building. The front view of the tower can be seen from the pend running down the side of the Queen's Hotel on the other side of the Nethergate. This was once the entry to the Palace Theatre, latterly taking the name of Dundee's original Theatre Royal, which was destroyed by fire in 1977 after lying empty for several years.

Morgan Tower and Nethergate. Dundee.

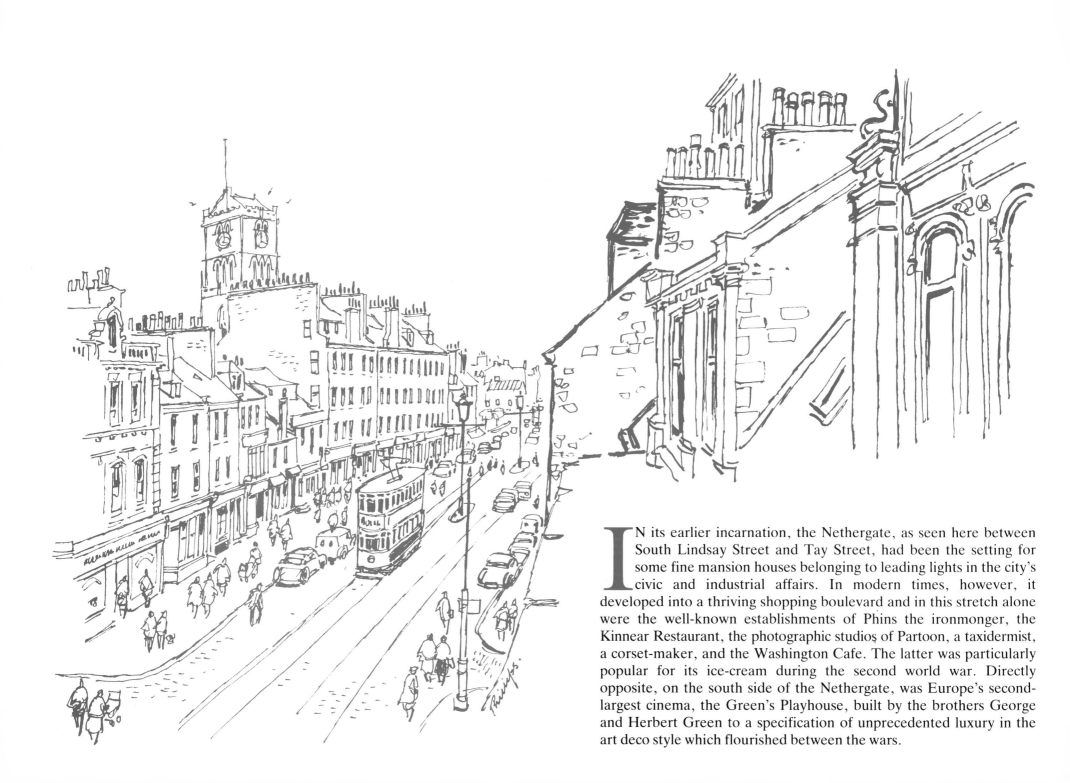

IN its earlier incarnation, the Nethergate, as seen here between South Lindsay Street and Tay Street, had been the setting for some fine mansion houses belonging to leading lights in the city's civic and industrial affairs. In modern times, however, it developed into a thriving shopping boulevard and in this stretch alone were the well-known establishments of Phins the ironmonger, the Kinnear Restaurant, the photographic studios of Partoon, a taxidermist, a corset-maker, and the Washington Cafe. The latter was particularly popular for its ice-cream during the second world war. Directly opposite, on the south side of the Nethergate, was Europe's second-largest cinema, the Green's Playhouse, built by the brothers George and Herbert Green to a specification of unprecedented luxury in the art deco style which flourished between the wars.

The more expensive seats in the huge auditorium were described as "golden divans," a favourite with courting couples, and in the spacious reception area there was a cafe with its own designer crockery. Today the Green's is a bingo hall, but at least the building lives on, which is more than can be said for almost all the other former cinemas in Dundee. Over 40 have come and gone since the first permanent one, called the Stobswell Cinema and Theatre, later renamed the Ritz, was opened in Morgan Street in 1910. The peak years for the cinema industry in the city were 1936-37 when over 30 picture houses were going full swing, offering more than 30,000 seats to a public more cinema conscious than any other community in Britain. The big, fashionable places were the Green's, King's, Kinnaird, La Scala, and the Majestic. But it was the smaller, sometimes backstreet, cinemas that evoke the greatest nostalgia with names like Rialto, Royalty, Broadway, Cinerama, Forest Park, Tivoli, Regent, Regal, and the "Vic". Before the talkies arrived in 1928 the larger houses had their own orchestras to provide the sound effects, with the more modest cinemas having only a "honky-tonk" pianist. In these days the projectionist could slow down or quicken up the speed of the film according to the time the manager wished the performance to last. But, of course, that bit of self-regulation ended with the introduction of sound.

One great controversy which still remains over Dundee's cinema era was admission by jam jars. Many swear that certain cinemas accepted "jeely" jars as the price of a seat. Others just as vehemently deny this, claiming the jars were exchanged for coppers at a grocer's shop with the proceeds then being used to purchase a ticket. It is agreed, however, that twopenny tea coupons could be bartered for a place in the stalls at some of the "flicks". Today there is only one full-time cinema left in Dundee and the cost of a ticket is £3.10p.

The West Port

THE West Port, at one time a principal gateway in Dundee's old defensive wall, later became a spacious concourse opening out from the top of the Overgate, but now largely destroyed by a new road system. Two thoroughfares, Hawkhill and Blackness Road, converged here from the densely-populated west end, allowing pedestrians a continuous downhill passage through Overgate into the city centre. On a busy Saturday people poured down this route like a river running towards the sea. Hawkhill, forking away on the left, home of the famous Harriers, is now largely a university precinct, whilst the new by-pass round this development has decimated Blackness Road.

Promenading, as in the Overgate, was a favourite past-time in this part of the city for the younger set, giving rise to the phrase: "Up the Hackie and doon the Blackie." Another custom, though not confined to the West Port area, involved women propping themselves up with a cushion at the open window of their tenement houses and leaning over the edge to survey the passing scene in the street below. Very often they would also have a blether with another woman further along the block or even on the floor below. This social convention was called, "a hingy oot". As in other parts of the inner city, the West Port district had its fair share of the squalor and slums which had been spawned by the 19th century industrialisation of Dundee. Its workers were among the poorest in Britain, the degradation of their overcrowded hovels in dire contrast to the palatial mansions of the jute barons spreadeagled across prime sites on the city outskirts. Between 1841 and 1861, for example, Dundee's population leaped by 30,000, yet in that period only 568 houses were built. By 1901, 72 per cent of the population lived in either single ends or room and kitchens.

But despite the urgent need for investment to upgrade these appalling social conditions at home, and eliminate the consequent disease, Dundee investors ploughed their money instead into the expansion of America following the Civil War, channelling £5 million within ten years into cattle, land, railways and ranching through a spate of local investment companies. The Dundee Mortgage and Trust Investment Co., set up in 1876, made loans of over a million dollars during its first

year through outlets in Chicago, San Francisco, and Indianapolis, but also benefiting the great farming territories of Iowa and Manitoba. Soon Dundee money was helping to prop up the economies of Missouri, Nebraska, Tennessee, Texas, Kentucky, New Mexico, and a host of other states. With returns of up to 12 per cent, compared to only 4 per cent at home, it was little wonder that the capitalists decided to export their wealth on a grand scale. Despite this, however, Dundee benefited greatly from the philanthrophy of its rich businessmen who provided the city with parks, educational and medical facilities, libraries, and many other public gifts.

POLICE boxes were a familiar feature of the Dundee landscape for nearly fifty years, a network of miniature police stations which the beat bobbies could call their own. There were eighty of them strategically placed round the city and, although of little architectural merit and even less comfort, they have left a lasting impression on both police and public.

Youngsters regarded the boxes with varying degrees of apprehension. A visit to the "cooler" for some minor infringement was enough to set most of them on a law-abiding course for the rest of their lives. There were, of course, exceptions. One little lad caught playing football in a Lochee street was taken to a box by the beat man to spill the beans on his pals who had escaped. When he refused to give their names the bobby said he would leave him in the box on his own for half an hour to think things over. But this tactic didn't work and the "prisoner" was duly released. The boy then ran a safe distance down the street before turning and shouting back defiantly at the constable: "No, e'm no tellin' yi their names. And whit's mare, eh've eaten yir piece"!

The boxes first appeared on the streets in 1935 with the closure of almost all district police stations, thus allowing sergeants and constables to go straight to their beats when reporting for duty. There were three types of boxes; section boxes to accommodate a sergeant and two constables, a beat box for one or two constables, and emergency boxes not much bigger than a telephone kiosk. At the time, these represented a great improvement in police efficiency. A flashing light on the roof of the box would alert the beat man to call headquarters immediately to receive fresh instructions and information. The public could also use the boxes for summoning help and reporting incidents. To do this a person would only have to pull open a small door in the wall of the box to be automatically connected to the switchboard at headquarters. A loudspeaker and microphone permitted a two-way conversation to be conducted from the pavement. The boxes, each kitted out with emergency tools and first aid supplies, also offered the bobbies a place of sanctuary for their meal breaks as well as providing a temporary holding post for those arrested and waiting transportation to Bell Street. The opening of modern sub-stations in the early 1960's, followed later by two-way personal radios and Panda cars, gradually phased out the "cans". The last one, at the junction of Strathmartine Road and Clepington Road, closed down in 1988. The day of the police box had passed into the pages of Dundee's history.

THEY were officially described as the public wash-houses and baths. But in a flash of immortal inspiration they were dubbed the "steamies", and it is as such they have been affectionately known ever since. From 1897 these communal washing centres, housed in substantial stone buildings which could have passed for libraries, formed a vital part of Dundee's domestic and social fabric. Their need, of course, arose from the appalling housing conditions of the city's industrial population, a community of tenement dwellers without proper sanitary or washing facilities. Soon it became a common sight to see women pushing pramfuls of laundry through the streets on their way to the "steamie". In Dundee they were located in most areas of the city including Constable Street, Caldrum Street, Miller's Wynd, Guthrie Street, and High Street, Lochee. Inside, the buildings were divided into two areas; one with tubs, wringers, pulleys, and boilers for washing clothes, the other lined with cubicles for those taking a bath. While the women boiled and scrubbed their wash, steam and condensation everywhere, the big halls rang to the sound of banter and gossip, a combination of blethering and lathering which turned this weekly chore into a kind of social jamboree.

Having a bath was, of course, a more private affair, although even here there was a very definite dialogue. The cubicles were numbered and the baths filled from a master set of taps controlled by an attendant, giving rise to shouts of, "More hot for Number Six", or "Can Number Two have a bit of cold"? The "steamie" was where you met friends and neighbours on a regular basis. It was also an outing for the bairns. But with modern housing, the mass production of washing machines, and the development of laundrettes, the "steamies" were gradually phased out, the last one closing in Dundee in the mid 1970's. There are those who still swear that the "steamie" could produce a whiter wash than any laundrette yet invented. This theory was tested by a television reporter when Perth's central wash-houses were threatened with closure in 1969. He washed two of his vests – one in the "steamie", the other in a laundrette – then, pinning them on a pole, asked passers-by to choose the whiter of the two.

The "steamie" emerged the winner, adding weight to a campaign by housewives which finally succeeded in keeping the wash-houses open for several more years. Now, if you want to recapture the atmosphere of such a place, you must visit the theatre and see the dramatised version in one of the most successful plays written in recent years, called simply, "The Steamie"

He has been widely described as "the writer of the world's worst bad verse". Nevertheless, his work has a vast international following and his idiosyncratic, almost naive, style of versifying his thoughts on a wide range of topical events has been hailed as having great literary merit by aficionados in many parts of the world. His Tay Bridge poem was possibly his most famous, but in this more mundane offering the poet shows his compassion for a fireman who has perished in a Dundee blaze:

"But brave James Fyffe held on to the hose till the last,
And when found in the debris, the people stood aghast.
When they saw him lying dead, with the hose in his hand,
Their tears for him they couldn't check nor yet command.

Oh heaven! I must confess it was no joke,
To see them struggling in the midst of suffocating smoke,
Each man struggling hard, no doubt, to save his life,
When he thought of his dear children and his wife . . .

But accidents will happen, by land and by sea,
Therefore, to save ourselves from accidents, we needn't try to flee,
For whatsoever God has ordained will come to pass;
For instance, ye might be killed by a stone or a piece of glass."

APPROACHING the city centre from the west brings you to the Sinderins, the point at which Perth Road continues into town on the right with Hawkhill forking off to the left, both thoroughfares wedged apart by a solid mass of tenements to form this gushet. Sinder is an old Scots word meaning "to sunder or part", thus Sinderins is the parting of the ways. Continuing along Perth Road we come to the birthplace of a man who, whatever else may be said about him, holds a unique place in the city's history. He is the controversial William McGonagall, poet and tragedian extraordinary. He was a handloom weaver living in Paton's Lane when the Muse first came to him in 1877 at the age of 52. From then until he died in 1902, McGonagall toured the country in wide brimmed hat and frock coat, reciting his torturous verse with great histrionics, believing himself to be the Poet Laureate and a man before his time. His celebrated journey to Balmoral Castle in 1878, where he arrived on foot, and on "spec", to perform before Queen Victoria, ended when he was turned back at the lodge gates. McGonagall was largely regarded as a figure of fun, a simple fellow who most people treated with patient indulgence.

William McGonagall died in penury at the age of 77, already a legend in his own lifetime, proving yet again that if you cannot be famous for being the best you can become almost as famous for being the worst. Today, McGonagall Suppers are now a regular event and there also exists a McGonagall Appreciation Society. The poet has become as synonymous with Dundee as jute, jam, or journalism, and yet Dundee has never really honoured his memory. There was word at one time of a statue at the Sinderins, but the only public acknowledgement so far of McGonagall's existence is in the name of a lounge bar in Perth Road. In view of his opposition to strong drink this would hardly have pleased him.

The Sinderins.

Whitehall Crescent
and the Old West Station, Dundee.

Douglas Phillips. ©

IN a city which had many fine landscapes this was one of the most striking, the opulent-looking West Station as framed within the gracious, curving lines of Whitehall Crescent. The impressive, towered baronial railway terminus was built in 1890 by the Caledonian company who had taken over the Dundee and Perth Railway twenty-five years before. The site had previously been occupied by Trinity House, the headquarters of the Fraternity of Masters and Seamen in Dundee, which at one time had considerable say in the running of the port. The West Station, later to become part of the L.M.S. network, waved off its last train on May 1, 1963. In 1966, after a public inquiry had heard impassioned pleas for its retention, possibly as a bus terminus, the station was demolished to make way for the inner ring road, the second time that the building on this ill-fated site in South Union Street had been reduced to rubble.

Whitehall Crescent, its corner sites once occupied by such familiar establishments as Justice, the house furnisher, Cantrell's fish shop, and Mather's Hotel, has still managed to survive, despite the wholesale demolition which has gone on all around it. Whitehall Street, linking High Street to the Crescent, had some of the best shops in town, including Draffen's department store; Henderson & Mackay, ladies outfitters; Larg's, the music sellers; and Kidd's book shop. But looking west down the Crescent today from the foot of Whitehall Street opens up an entirely different, aesthetically barren, prospect as a contemporary drawing of the view shows only too clearly. Now there is a foot bridge running from the Nethergate Centre and the bottom of Union Street across the Inner Ring Road to Tay Bridge Station, marooned in a flow of traffic.

ALTHOUGH ferry boats had been criss-crossing the Tay for several centuries, it wasn't until Dundee Harbour Trust took over the service in 1873 that the "Fifies" were run on a proper commercial basis. Sail had been supplanted by steam in 1821 and during the next 145 years of powered ferries thirteen ships were built to ply the route between Newport Harbour and Craig Pier, at the foot of South Union Street, Dundee. The big, squat vessels, crammed with passengers and vehicles, ingrained themselves in the affections of all who sailed in them. The crossing of just under two miles could take anything from twenty to forty minutes, depending on wind and tide, and with a uniformed captain on the bridge and throbbing engines below it was the nearest many youngsters ever got to being on a cruise ship. Their Sunday picnics on the braes of Newport were a thankful break from the tenement-lands of industrial Dundee. A ticket for the crossing only allowed you on the the deck of the "Fifie", a seat in the saloon being extra, although many of the regulars going to work in Dundee each day promenaded round the deck as a form of exercise during the "voyage". Latterly the big names of the fleet were the Sir William High, named after a Lord Provost, the B.L. Nairn, the last of the "paddlers", and the Scotscraig and Abercraig. The last two, with their increased capacity for carrying vehicles, were the regular ferries during the final fifteen years of the service which ended on August 18, 1966, the same day as the Queen Mother had officially opened the Tay Road Bridge.

The "Fifies" provided a faithful service across the Tay and although there were several incidents of passengers and vehicles slipping into the water, not one of the vessels was involved in a total shipwreck. There were, however, one or two narrow squeaks. On a dark and foggy night in December, 1948, the Sir William High, the only Fifie at that time without radar, couldn't find Craig Pier and became stranded on the Fowler Rock, off the Western Pier. It was carrying a heavy load of cars and listing badly. Fears that the vessel might overturn didn't materialise but Broughty lifeboat had to ferry seventy passengers to safety. Then, in July 1964, the Abercraig was swept in a gale against the temporary bridge serving as a platform for the building of the main road crossing. Passengers were assisted on to the spidery framework and then walked along a beam to the Dundee shore. The last crossing in August, 1966, was undertaken by the Scotscraig, smothered in bunting and packed to the gunwhales with passengers from both sides of the river. A band on board played a selection of tunes and hymns, a religious service was conducted during the crossing, and as the vessel tied up at Craig Pier there was a spirited rendition of "Auld Lang Syne". As with the last farewell to the trams before them, the "Fifies" bowed out in a sea of emotion.

B.L. Nairn
Dundee Tay Ferries.

Douglas Phillips.

THE west end of Dock Street, skirting Earl Grey Dock and finishing opposite the West Station, was always a hive of activity, a confluence of several streets sending a stream of buses, cars, and horse-drawn carts into this bottom part of the town. Large crowds would make their way to Craig Street market, just off to the left, and the Dock Street Dining Rooms on the corner, which offered good, plain fare for over a hundred years, was another popular attraction. Across the road, between the Whitehall Bar and Mather's Hotel, was the wholesale fruit warehouse of Harrison and Reeve. At the top end of Earl Grey Dock, beside the original swimming baths, was Britain's oldest warship afloat, H.M.S. Unicorn, a wooden-walled frigate which came to Dundee in 1873 and is now moored in Victoria Dock.

The Unicorn, long since roofed over, was launched in 1824, only nineteen years after the Battle of Trafalgar, and although armed with 46 guns she never fired any in anger. This elevated view of Dock Street takes in the Tay Bridge and no story about old Dundee would be complete without reference to the calamity which befell one of the most famous railway crossings in the world. The bridge, built by Thomas Bouch, was hailed as an engineering miracle, its two-mile span making it the longest ever built across water at that time. Bouch was rewarded with a knighthood and the Freedom of Dundee. McGonagall, however, struck a cautionary note in what was to become his best known poem:

"Beautiful Railway Bridge of the Silvery Tay!
I hope that God will protect all passengers
By night and by day.
And that no accident will befall them while crossing
The bridge of the Silvery Tay,
For that would be most awful to be seen
Near by Dundee and the Magdalen Green."

But on a night of hurricane winds in December, 1879, only nineteen months after going into service, McGonagall's fear came to pass when the centre section of the bridge collapsed into the boiling river, taking with it a train and its 75 passengers and crew, all of whom perished. The inquiry later concluded that the bridge had been badly designed, constructed and maintained. Bouch died a broken man within a year of the disaster. Eight years later a new Tay Bridge had been built alongside the piers of its ill-fated predecessor. But the drama and infamy of the original bridge lives on to this day.

West Dock St.
Dundee

SELDECK STREET DINING ROOMS

THE WHITEHALL

Douglas Phillips.

The Royal Arch
Dundee

Douglas Phillips.

DUNDEE Town Council went bankrupt in 1842, largely as a result of overspending on the repair and maintenance of the city churches over the previous thirteen years, expenditure which proved to be money thrown away when the churches were destroyed by fire in 1841. As a result of this insolvency, which lasted for 22 years, the quality public buildings of the period were financed by private capital and designed by first-class architects from outside the town. The Royal Arch in Dock Street, straddling the King William and Earl Grey Docks and seen here from the foot of Crichton Street, was an example of this privatisation policy at the time. Its design was the subject of a competition won by a Glasgow architect, J. T. Rochead, and the construction of the giant neo-Norman triumphal arch in 1851 was funded by subscription at a cost of nearly £3000. The arch was built to commemorate the visit to Dundee seven years earlier by Queen Victoria, Prince Albert, and the Princess Royal, who had stepped ashore from the royal yacht on their way north for a highland holiday. For that actual occasion, September 11, 1844, the harbour engineer, James Leslie, had designed a temporary arch made of wood which was then hastily put into position. But its permanent stone replacement, to become one of the city's most notable landmarks, was knocked down in 1964 to make way for the Tay Road Bridge approaches. The Royal Arch faced across dock Street to a spacious concourse which was later developed into the Shore Terrace bus terminus, but in earlier times was occupied by the highly popular Greenmarket, described as follows in the records of 1873:

"This quarter of the town is greatly frequented on Saturday evenings, the attractions being of an extremely varied and diverse character. In close juxtaposition may be seen the street preacher addressing the crowd, the quack doctor vending his nostrums, the cheap John and the ballad-singer, galvanic batteries, beef and sweetie stands, and exhibitions of dead and living wonders, forming altogether a curious medley, which cannot fail to give a stranger a curious glimpse into one of the most singular phases of Dundee life."

With two of Dundee's docks lying hard against the public thoroughfare it was a common sight to see vessels bobbing at anchor at the edge of the street. The one shown here in Earl Grey Dock belonged to a fleet of sandboats run by various companies. They were licenced to extract nearly 200,000 tons of sand each year from various deposits in the river, much of it provided by the Middlebank lying between the bridges. Most of the sand was used in concrete and cement, but when these docks were filled in for the bridge the sand boats went into decline and now the raw material is taken from other sources.

WHEN Dundee developed into a major port in the 19th century, its trading tentacles reaching out to most parts of the world, the road system leading to the docks was greatly expanded. This improved access to the harbour was focussed on Dock Street itself which now became the town's main commercial artery and later still, with the advent of trains and buses, the centre of Dundee's transport network. In 1932, Shore Terrace, once the site of the Greenmarket, then became the Corporation bus terminus. From here the public fleet of double and single deckers in their green and white livery radiated to every part of the city. During the next 42 years this area between the foot of Castle Street and Crichton Street became the daily dispersal point for thousands of Dundonians, creating a lucrative retail trade at the bottom end of the town.

City Arcade

The City Arcade, built into the rear of the Caird Hall building at street level, was particularly convenient for the commuters with its wide range of stalls, including an amusement centre, crushed together under the one roof with its own distinctive atmosphere. Dundee's three railway stations were also located within the Dock Street area, the West and Taybridge Stations being in South Union Street and the East Station, less than a mile away, in Dock Street itself. When the East opened in 1840 it was the city's only rail route to Aberdeen and the north and by the turn of the century was handling 80 trains a day from five in the morning until eleven at night. When the rail tunnel was laid below Dock Street, circa 1880, linking the Taybridge and East Stations, the Aberdeen line later became part of the L.N.E.R. network and the East concentrated on short-haul routes up the coast to Arbroath before closing in January 1959. As if all this traffic activity wasn't enough, there was also a railway line running along the surface of Dock Street, going from the Harbour to the sidings in South Union Street. This was used by a puffer engine and wagons preceded by a man on foot with a red warning flag. Next to the Royal Arch stood the Empress Ballroom, a popular night spot for twenty-five years, particularly during the war when it became a favourite mustering point for visiting servicemen. The Empress stood at the side of King William Dock, the anchorage for Dundee's sprat boats. Sprats resembled large sardines and were netted in the river between Tayport and the Rail bridge. At one time forty yawls worked these grounds but after 1945 the fleet of twenty small, engine-powered boats was gradually reduced until sprat fishing from Dundee ended in the late 1950's after a local cannery had been relocated in the north of Scotland. Almost everything in this scene has disappeared, sacrificed on the high alter of the road bridge. Two classical monuments, however, still remain. The Merchant's Exchange, with library and assembly rooms, built in Shore Terrace in 1828 and later to become a masonic temple, has for long now been the printing works of David Winter and Son Ltd. The other survivor is the Customs House, the largest in Scotland when it opened in 1842 at the Harbour entrance on the other side of King William Dock, with the East Station almost alongside. On the following two pages the juxtaposition of the docks to mainland Dundee give the city a charming, almost Venetian, aspect.

Dock Street and Old Harbour Dundee.

Douglas Phillips ©

Phillips

Dundee docks
The Inner Basin.

Phieups
Dock Street Dundee

IT was jute that finally put Dundee on the map in the second half of the 19th century, giving the city international status as the world's largest centre for manufacturing the raw Indian fibre and forging strong economic links between Dundee on the Tay and Calcutta on the Hooghly. By 1873 Dundee was a city of tall, smoking chimneys with 72 mills and factories giving jobs to over 42,000 of its people, spinning and weaving miles of cloth as quickly as the jute liners could unload their bulging cargoes. The city's textile industry had previously been based on flax and linen. But with war in the Crimea and civil conflict in America it was cheaper and tougher jute that took the ascendancy as contracts rolled in for gun covers, tarpaulin, tenting, and sand bags. The accelerating demand for jute products reshaped the social and economic structure of Dundee, multiplying the population, exacerbating the already chronic shortage of decent housing, and widening the gulf between rich and poor. It was the women who took the brunt of the daily grind in the mills and factories with more than half of the city's workers being drawn from the female ranks. Jute also created a golden age of mill building, industrial architecture which has handed down names never to be forgotten; Eagle, Bowbridge, Manhattan, South Mills, Ashton, Craigie, Victoria, Dura, Heathfield, Hillbank . . . the litany is never ending. The jute barons included the families of Gilroy, Grimmond, Cox and Baxter. But two of the most notable names to emerge from this era of jute were a couple of mill girls whose concern for the exploited and under-privileged led them, in totally different ways, to seek justice through sacrifice. Mary Slessor, her faith rooted in the Word of God, sailed off to darkest Africa to become a famous missionary in Calabar. Mary Brooksbank, motivated by militant atheism, stayed at home to campaign, and be jailed, for her struggle to improve conditions for the unemployed, the ill-fed and the badly housed. In the book of verse and song she left behind were her famous lines:

> "Oh, dear me, the mill's gaen fest,
> The puir wee shifters canna get a rest,
> Shiftin' bobbins, coorse and fine,
> They fairly mak' ye work for your ten and nine."

Today Dundee's textile industry is no longer dependant on jute. But it was jute that first made Dundee really famous.

JOHN SMITH

FRUIT AND POTATO MERCHANTS

THE CAIRD ARMS

Crichton Street
Dundee.

Douglas Phillips. ©

CRICHTON Street was cut from High Street to Dock Street in 1820 to give greater access to an expanding Harbour. But the operation faced a difficulty beyond the normal parameters of civil engineering. Legend claims that an occupied house lay in the path of the proposed thoroughfare. It belonged to Dr John Crichton, son of local bailie, Thomas Crichton, who was reluctant to vacate his fine town residence. Negotiations were duly entered into and finally the good doctor agreed to sell his property to the Council, provided the new street carried his name, and so Crichton Street was born. The garage sign on the right indicates the well-known underground premises which run below the City Square, while across the street the Caird Arms give a clue to the identity of one of Dundee's greatest benefactors, Sir James Caird. His wealth came from the family jute manufacturing company of Cairds, established by his father Edward, with Ashton Works in Hawkhill and Craigie Works in Robertson Street. Sir James bestowed his munificence on many public projects, creating a trust fund which purchased Mains Estate, now Caird Park, along with Camperdown House and Park. He gifted his personal and very valuable Egyptian collection to the city museum and he donated £24,000 to Shackleton's 1914 expedition to the Antartic, the famous explorer having previously established a Dundee connection by standing as a candidate in the city at the Parliamentary elections in 1906.

But the name of the jute baron lives on most conspicuously through the Caird Hall, a long colonnaded building which dominates the City Square in the very heart of Dundee. Sir James gave £100,000 for its construction. It was designed by the city architect, James Thomson, to a brief devoid of grandeur, the foundation stone being laid in 1914 but final completion delayed by war until 1922. The colonnade was gifted by Caird's sister, after whom the appended Marryat Hall was given her married name. With an auditorium capable of seating almost 3000, the Caird Hall has been the venue of countless concerts, from classical to pop, as well as accommodating exhibitions, boxing and wrestling promotions, public lectures, and grand social occasions. Sir Thomas Beecham, once conducting in the hall, invited anyone who wasn't enjoying the concert to throw Dundee marmalade at him – provided they first removed it from the jar! Many years later the famous American entertainer, Danny Kaye, wandered on to the stage at the start of his performance and, shielding his eyes as if gazing into a distant horizon, shouted: "Hey you, at the back in Perth!" The Caird Hall has also witnessed many moments of high political drama over the past 70 years. This is where the votes are counted and results announced in local and general elections. It is from here the winning candidates set out for the corridors of power.

Cowgate and King St.
Dundee.

Douglas Phillips.

THE Cowgate had the traditional urban lay-out of tenements – shops on the ground floor and houses above – access to the flats being gained through closes and up rear flights of stairs. This popular combination of business and living premises ensured a human presence in the city centre round the clock, a piece of social engineering only properly appreciated after the second world war when central redevelopment and peripheral housing estates gradually turned inner Dundee into a ghost town during the night. The north side of Cowgate was part of this reconstruction, the tenements being replaced by the modern frontage of the new Wellgate shopping mall.

Along this stretch at the top of the Murraygate there was once Miss Hodge, the house furnishers; the costumiers, Style and Mantle; and Winning, the butcher. Across the road was Dundee's renowned King's Theatre, which opened in 1909, bringing to the city such big names as Marie Lloyd, Harry Lauder, and George Robey, besides staging the impressive productions of national touring companies including Sadler's Wells Opera. In 1950 it became the Gaumont, by 1961 it was a full-time cinema, and in 1981, now called the Odeon, it was closed. Today this treasure-house of memories is a bingo hall. Going eastwards along Cowgate either takes you up King Street by the old tram route or along the other fork to East Port. It is here you come across one of Dundee's ancient outlets, the Wishart Arch, named after the famous religious reformer, George Wishart, whose electrifying sermons from the parapet of the gate and elsewhere in the city built up considerable fervour for change in the established Catholic church. But in 1546, shortly after leaving Dundee to continue his preaching and work among the poor and sick in other parts of Scotland, Wishart was arrested and taken to St. Andrews where he was handed over to his implacable enemy Cardinal Bethune. Following a mock trial Wishart was led from his prison to the Castle Green where his execution had been arranged. While chained to the stake he kissed the cheek of his executioner and said: "Take this as a token that I forgive thee – do thine office." The brushwood round his legs was then kindled and within minutes the flames had ignited the powder fastened to his waist. Soon the scorched and mangled body of the brave reformer was reduced to ashes.

Today the Wishart Arch still stands in its original location, having survived regular collisions with passing vehicles and threats to have it dismantled and put up elsewhere. Wishart Memorial Church in King Street, the kirk attended by missionary Mary Slessor, also perpetuated the great man's name, although now it is a building used for other purposes.

The Wellgate Steps

THE Wellgate, bustling with life and full of character, was in many ways a smaller edition of the Overgate. It had a similar mix of houses and shops and, with its own resident cast of personalities, this narrow thoroughfare running from Victoria Road (left) down to Murraygate (right) was always one of the liveliest spots in town. Every Saturday, for example, a lovely Shetland pony was paraded over the cobbles, decked out in a blue silken cloth with a slogan emblazoned in large, red lettering: "Barrie – First in the Field." This was the 1910 advertising gimmick of Barrie, the outfitter, who specialised in football jerseys at 6s 6d a dozen (about 33 pence). Football was a recurring theme in the retail life of the Wellgate with two of the other shopkeepers being ardent supporters of Dundee F.C. Tom Gardiner, the tailor, offered a new overcoat to any Dundee player who scored two or more goals in a match, while Adam Piggot, the butcher, presented the team's goalkeeper with a choice roast every time he kept a clean sheet at Dens Park. This latter offer led to a chorus whenever Billy Muir conceded a goal, the crowd chanting: "Hard lines, Billy. Nae roast for yer denner the morn."! Near the bottom of the Wellgate there was Kerr's Boot Shop where children from poor families were supplied with free footwear on the authorisation of the School Board. There were other concessions, too, for those in need. A baker offered "olders" – unsold scones and pastries from the previous day – and on a Saturday night, in an old hall in Bain Square, there were penny concerts. The Wellgate takes its name from the Lady Well in this area, one of Dundee's three main sources of water until the middle of the 19th century. At the top of the street were the famous Wellgate steps, put there to negotiate the sudden, severe incline up to Victoria Road, and in time becoming, like The Pillars and Samuel's Corner, one of the great trysting places in the city. A girl asked up to dance by someone from out of town would sometimes say: "I can't really do this one, but I can give you the steps of the Wellgate." Today the Wellgate has been transformed beyond all recognition, being completely encased in a big shopping mall on three floors with an adjacent library complex and civic Steps Theatre, named after the flight of steps which had proved such a feature in the original layout.

The Wellgate

THE Hilltown, rising steeply above the Wellgate, was at one time the main route north and east out of Dundee, but this changed with the opening up of Victoria Road and King Street which provided gentler exits from the town. Nevertheless, the Hilltown, funnelling down into the Wellgate, continued to provide a natural pedestrian route leading to the city centre, in much the same way as Hawkhill and Blackness Road had once drained into the Overgate. The Hilltown had its fair share of character in both buildings and people. There was the Plaza Cinema and the Progress Dance Hall, known to all as the "Progy", and dining rooms at the foot of the Hill which specialised in tripe suppers. There was also the ancient Windmill Bar, which caught the eye of the Duke of Edinburgh as his car swept down the Hill during a royal visit to the city in May, 1977.

THE WINDMILL BAR

Customers saw him pointing out their howff to the Queen and later sent the Duke a piece of verse in which they asked him what exactly he had said about the bar. Much to everyone's surprise the Duke responded, also in poetic vein:

> "I recall very well the pub on the Hill
> Which now I see was the old Windmill,
> It wasn't the crowd coming out the door
> That caught my eye at quarter past four,
> T'was the Ann Street windows attracted my stare
> I wondered if anyone could be living up there,
> Then seeing the smiles on your customers' faces
> I reckoned your pub was one of those places,
> Where the noise of good cheer drives off all dull cares
> And makes it impossible to live up those stairs."

The Muse, in fact, seems to have stalked the Hilltown in many guises. McGonagall gave readings there and others on the Hill were also known to speak in verse. One of these was Sandy Soutar, the coalman who operated from a shed up a narrow white-washed close. He was a small, wiry man who, despite his occupation, preferred wearing white canvas shoes at work rather than tackety boots. Whenever a customer complained about the quality of his coal he would give them the standard reply:

> "When you buy the fish,
> You buy the banes.
> When you buy the coal,
> You buy the stanes."

The Hilltown was originally a ribbon development of houses on the Scrymgeour estate, a Barony outwith the jurisdiction of Dundee until sold to the town at the end of the 17th century. Its earlier name of Bonnethill arose from the main activity of the residents, that of knitting woollen bonnets. The bonnetmakers would sit on the street where they "wrought their bonnets with large wires". This, in fact, became one of the crafts included in the Nine Incorporated Trades, a guildry formed in 1575 for the mutual protection of employers and still existing today, but without the privileges it once exercised in running civic affairs.

HAIRDRESSER

Douglas Phillips.

Foot o' The Hill.

Douglas Phillips.

Top o' the Hill Dundee

THE top of the Hilltown, known simply as "Tap o' the Hill", is still the junction of several busy streets dominated by yet another prominent Dundee landmark, the Hilltown clock. Every Saturday during the football season thousands of fans check their watches against this faithful time-piece as they hurry towards kick-off at the nearby Dundee and Dundee United grounds. This was also a popular part of the town for jute mills and it was said that anyone living in this area was within earshot of the hooters, or "bummers", of nearly a dozen mills, all sounding off at starting and finishing times each working day. Although in this scene the street lighting had gone over to electricity with long, slender standards and automatic ignition, the era of the lamp-post and leerie was one which characterised street life in Dundee for well over fifty years. The leeries were employed by the Town Council to light and extinguish the gas lamps in the streets and tenement staircases, using a long pole with an eternal flame. Each leerie was allocated a beat which usually took him one and a half hours to cover twice a day, the balance of his shift being worked at the Lighting Department Depot. In his book, "Oor Dundee", the late David Phillips describes how a leerie was standing on the platform of a moving tram, holding his pole in the vertical position, when a policeman, sprinting to board the car between stops, grabbed the pole to pull himself aboard thinking it was the staunchion at the doorway. Within seconds both leerie and Bobby were doing backward sommersaults along the street!:

"Now Tom would be a driver and Maria go to sea,
And my papa's a banker and as rich as he can be;
But I, when I am stronger and can choose what I'm to do,
Oh Leerie, I'll go round at night and light the lamps with you"!

But the lamp-posts, or "lampies", did much more than illuminate the streets. They provided youngsters at play with a vital piece of furniture for their various games. The lampie could be the wickets for cricket or the goalposts for football. It was a gymnastic aid for those who wanted to climb and perform movements from the cross-bar, and by tying a skipping rope to the upper brackets the girls could play "round and round the Maypole". For others it was the ideal "block" for hide and seek. Street games were never the same again when they finally took away the lamp-posts.

TENEMENT building in Dundee went through a boom period towards the end of the 19th century as the city's population rapidly increased with the expansion of the jute trade. These industrial housing blocks were usually four storeys high, sometimes with a wooden stair on the top floor leading to a further row of garrets. Most of the houses were single ends, room and kitchen, or perhaps two-roomed, but invariably they were badly over-crowded with lavatories on the common stair being shared by several families. The houses were all entered from the rear of the building, with those above ground level having their doors opening on to long outside platforms, known as "pletties", which were connected to the main stairway.

Each tenement had its backcourt, sometimes with a bit of drying green, and it was here in the "backies" or the "greenies" that families intermingled, the children with their games and concerts and the mothers and fathers to pass the time of day in conversation. These communal areas resembled an ampitheatre, a vast stage above which the landings were tiered like the upper circles of an opera house. It was into such an arena that the itinerant street entertainers would come with their various acts, playing to an audience of tenants ranged along the pletties. These artistes were mainly singers and musicians of every description, bringing with them a vast range of instruments; accordions, fiddles, drums, banjoes, mouth organs, tin whistles, bugles, trumpets, and bagpipes. There was the occasional hurdy-gurdy – a mechanical piano on wheels – and even a horned gramophone pushed about in an old pram. At the end of each performance the entertainer would bow to the gallery and, impoverished though they might have been, the spectators would throw down their coins in appreciation. If money was a bit short the performer would get a bit of food. They would rarely leave the "stage" without something. Several of these buskers were disabled ex-servicemen who wore their ribbons and medals.

But the most memorable of all was Martha Wallace, a small, blind woman with a fine, resonant voice which, in different circumstances, might have been heard in more fashionable circles. She was known to everyone as "Blind Mattie", a real star who brought tears to the eyes with such numbers as "My Ain Wee Hoose" and "Hame o' Mine". Born without sight in Kirriemuir, Martha came to Dundee with her parents as a young girl and later took up singing to earn a living. She accompanied herself on the melodeon and in a successful week could pick up nearly £4 – as much as a good tradesman at that time. Blind Mattie kept up her musical rounds, going as far afield as Broughty Ferry and Invergowrie, until she was 70. She died in 1962 at the age of 86 in The Rowans, an old folks' home in the east end of the city. At her funeral there were floral tributes from the Lord Provost and other leading figures in city life.

Douglas Phillips.

The High St. Lochee.

DESPITE becoming part of Dundee in 1859, the village of Lochee continued to maintain an identity of its own although now, like all the old suburbs, it has been swamped in a sea of post-war development. The High Street itself did not escape in this time of massive change, almost the entire frontage on the left or west side, as seen here, having been replaced with modern arcades. Lochee's prosperity was traditionally based on jute, by courtesy of the Cox dynasty which built a vast manufacturing complex on 30 acres just behind the east side of the High Street and entered near the clock-towered East Church which was knocked down in 1960. At one time these Camperdown Works employed over 5000 people and formed the biggest jute operation in the world. Here they had their own railway siding and a foundry with eighteen forges. The site also boasted of something else – a magnificent 282-foot-high mosaic brick chimney designed by local architect James MacLaren in 1866. Cox's Stack, as it became known, is still one of the poshest lums in the land and can be seen on a clear day from the 4000-foot summit of Ben Lawers on the far shores of Loch Tay, fifty miles away. The Camperdown site is now being redeveloped but the famous stack stands on, protected from the demolisher's dynamite by being designated a listed building. The Cox family also gave generously to the community, Lochee Park being one of their gifts and James Cox serving as provost of Dundee from 1872 to 1875. In these days Lochee was largely populated by Irish immigrants who had flooded into the town to escape the Famine and seek work in the local textile factories. Many of them in Lochee were housed in a complex of tenements which became known as Tipperary. Hansom cabs were also much in evidence in this part of the city, a regular service being offered by Valentine's Stables in the High Street. But it was local milkman Archie Gow who had the most intelligent horse in town. It didn't even require a driver. When Archie lost track of time in the West End Bar in Liff Road at the end of his morning round the horse, complete with cart, simply trotted back on its own to the dairy in Buttar's Loan. They always were self-sufficient in Lochee.

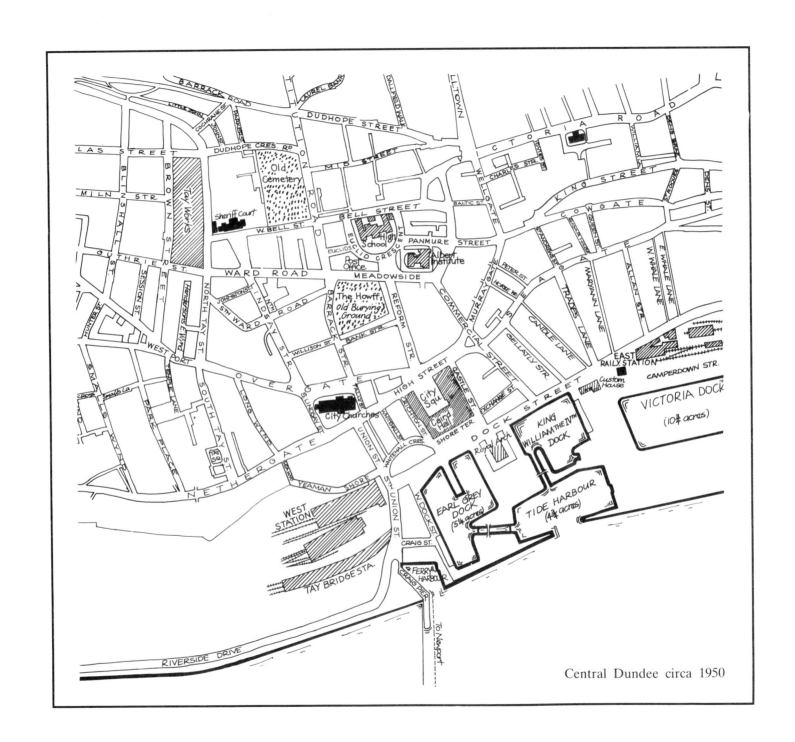

Central Dundee circa 1950

"The Pillars"